POOR WHITE TRASH

From a Pauper to a Child of the King

JIM MARLOW

ISBN 979-8-89309-695-8 (Paperback)
ISBN 979-8-89309-790-0 (Hardcover)
ISBN 979-8-89309-696-5 (Digital)

Copyright © 2024 Jim Marlow
All rights reserved
First Edition

All scripture quotations are taken from the King James Version.

All rights reserved. No part of this publication may be reproduced, distributed, or transmitted in any form or by any means, including photocopying, recording, or other electronic or mechanical methods without the prior written permission of the publisher. For permission requests, solicit the publisher via the address below.

Covenant Books
11661 Hwy 707
Murrells Inlet, SC 29576
www.covenantbooks.com

To my Lord and Savior, Jesus Christ.
To my loving family.

Our righteousness are as filthy rags.

—Isaiah 64:6

CONTENTS

Introduction ix
Part 1: Poor White Trash 1
    Chapter 1: Poor White Trash 3
    Chapter 2: Hard Work and Sacrifices 5
    Chapter 3: Making a Living 7
    Chapter 4: Momma 8
    Chapter 5: Conditioning 10
    Chapter 6: Fight or Flight—Choosing My Battles…Wisely? ... 13
    Chapter 7: A Taste of Wealth 15
    Chapter 8: Visitors 17
    Chapter 9: Fire on the Mountain 19
    Chapter 10: Winter Woes 20
    Chapter 11: Replenishing 21
    Chapter 12: The Calling 22
    Chapter 13: From a Boy to a Man 24
    Chapter 14: Ignorance 26
    Chapter 15: Getting My Wings 27
    Chapter 16: The Nut Doesn't Fall Far from the Tree 29
    Chapter 17: Deployment 30
    Chapter 18: Join the Military, See the World 31
    Chapter 19: Be All You Can Be 35
    Chapter 20: Mistaken Identity 37
    Chapter 21: Countdown 39
    Chapter 22: Civilian Life 41
    Chapter 23: Close Call 42
    Chapter 24: Snowstorm of Love 44
    Chapter 25: What Is Love? (A Little Free Advice) 46

Part 2: From a Pauper to a Child of the King 47
    Chapter 26: Back in Church…Sort Of 49
    Chapter 27: Studying for the Tests 51
    Chapter 28: Family or Fame? 53
    Chapter 29: When the Wind Blows, Raise Your Sail 55
    Chapter 30: Taking the Test 56
    Chapter 31: God of the Hills and the Valleys 60
    Chapter 32: Turn That Frown Upside Down 63
    Chapter 33: Crooked Justice 68
Epilogue 71
Acknowledgments 73

INTRODUCTION

CONGRATULATIONS TO YOU for buying my book.

I have heard so many men blame their current bad behavior on their past—how they were treated when they were a child, how mean people were to them, being raised in a single-parent home or by no parents at all, how they never got what they wanted, or how poor they were growing up. I am living proof that there is a God who wants better for us, and He sees us, no matter where we are and what we are going through. He can make us into so much more than what any parent or boss or situation could ever try to make us out to be. He can truly turn a pauper into a child of the King! What Satan tries to destroy, God *can* turn it around for our good.

Satan tried so many times to destroy me, but my heavenly Father had plans for me. He called out to me, and I answered. I was not perfect. I am still a work in progress.

PART 1

Poor White Trash

CHAPTER 1

Poor White Trash

WE WILL TALK about that title later.

I was born Jimmy Odell Marlow on November 8, 1944. Of course, I don't remember that day, although it seems I can remember *almost* that far back.

I know times were hard back then, just after World War II. But what I don't understand is, they didn't get any better until I was grown, which brings me to a very important point in life.

Life is what you make it to be. I didn't learn this or most other things from a book. I learned it from the hard knocks of life, knowledge I will never forget. I don't understand when I see people in handcuffs saying, "I never had a chance in life," or "I was raised in the brickyards," meaning low-income projects. Where I came from, that would have been a boost in life. I don't think they had low-income housing in those days. If we were fortunate enough to have lived in a place like that, I would have felt like the most privileged kid in the world.

We lived in old houses, where there was no insulation, and sometimes there wasn't even sealed walls or ceilings. I have been sitting there and have had a snake fall from the rafters. On one occasion, a copperhead snake was in my bed, and on another occasion, there was a stinging scorpion in my bed!

We kept a barrel under the edge of the roof to catch rainwater. When a spark came out of the stovepipe, it would usually catch the wooden shingles on fire, and we would use the water that we caught in the rain barrel to put the fire out. This happened frequently. We had to keep a fire going year-round because we cooked on a wood stove in the kitchen. We must have lived in at least twenty different houses. You might have called them shacks when I was a kid. But I don't want to hear how hard it was growing up in your concrete jungle and brickyards. At least they had running water, heat, and electricity.

In one place where we lived, there was a well where we drew the water up with a bucket and a rope, but in most of the places we lived, we had to carry water from a nearby spring to use for drinking, cooking, bathing, and washing clothes. Don't get me started on going to the toilet at midnight on a cold, winter night!

CHAPTER 2

Hard Work and Sacrifices

I GUESS MOST of you don't know what a crosscut saw or a chopping axe is. I can spell it out for you—*hard work*! No wood, no heat. No wood, no eat. Plain and simple. Chopping wood was an everyday chore. Even when the temperature outside was well over one hundred degrees.

We didn't have grocery stores that we could run to get food. if we didn't grow it, we killed it and ate it. I know you, animal rights lovers, might get mad at me for the next part of this paragraph, but I have always loved animals. Most of them were fine eating. If it hadn't been for the wild animals that God gave us, we surely would have starved. "Thank You, Lord."

I am seventy-six years old as I write this. Thanks to all those wonderful animals who made it possible by sacrificing their lives for me.

Thanks be to my Father in heaven for giving His Son, Jesus Christ, who gave His life to save my soul.

We all make sacrifices, from my heavenly Father to the animals, with mankind in the middle. Many is the time growing up that I went to bed hungry when the hunting was no good. We relied on the creeks for food also. We would fish with a hook and line. We would seine the creek, which is to use a net. We would gig the fish at night while using a miner's lamp to see. Sometimes, if we could get some dynamite, we would blow the creek, anything for a meal. It was a matter of survival other than stealing. That's one thing my mom drew the line on. We ate frog legs, squirrels, rabbits, raccoons, ground hogs, and several different kinds of birds and occasionally a wild hog. They were very rarely found though. If you are hungry, you will eat about anything and do about anything to get it.

In Middle Tennessee, where I was brought up, there were no deer or turkey. They had all been killed out by people as poor as we were. Once in a blue moon, a black bear might be seen.

Now, there is an abundance of game. Sometimes I sit and watch rabbits, deer, and turkeys in my yard. There are so many squirrels that I almost have to kick them out from under my feet. They fed me when I was young. Now I feed them. Don't get me wrong though; I still like a smoked shoulder of deer every now and then.

CHAPTER 3

Making a Living

I CAME FROM and around a small town called Sherwood. If you counted all the people and their dogs, it wouldn't amount to five hundred.

When I was growing up, the major source of income was from making or bootlegging moonshine. If you weren't making it, you were bootlegging it.

We never came up with enough material or money to start a moonshine operation. I don't think Mom would have allowed that anyway. She had a lot of morals in one way. In other ways—well, you figure that out. I know she was the head of our household, and what she said was the law.

A friend of mine, who is an engineer, just drew up the plans for Jack Daniels to double their distillery in size. When he finished, he said, "Jim, I now know how to make whiskey." I said, "Sam, if you had asked me, I could have told you and saved you a lot of money you spent on engineering school!"

Moonshining was as common as spring water, and most of the people I knew drank it like water. Some members of my family would give me whiskey when I was so small that it was unbelievable. I was drunk before I was of school age. It makes me shudder to think of the things that went on. They thought it was funny to see a five-year-old staggering around. It's only by God's grace that it didn't kill me. God had a plan for me though. It would be several years down the road before I knew what that plan was.

CHAPTER 4

Momma

I OWE MY soul to my heavenly Father. Tell me, Lord, and I will go. Show me, Lord, and I will do.

I was born to a woman who I really can't describe. She had five children by her first husband, who died early in his life. The things I have been told by my mom and several others is he was a mean man who beat her and the children. I guess he wouldn't work much so she had to do whatever she could to feed her children. If he didn't like what she put on the table, he would throw it on the floor and beat her. She would fight back, but that just made it worse for her. She was a small woman and couldn't match his strength. On one occasion, when she was about seven months pregnant with her third child, he put the barrel of a twelve-gauge shotgun in her belly and pulled the trigger. The gun snapped. The next day, her only male child took the same gun and same shell hunting and killed a rabbit.

My mom grew to be a very hard-hearted woman. I guess she wound up hating the world. I think, by the time I was born, she had rather fought than eat. Her husband died after five children, and she took in washings on a rubboard and ironings for people that could afford it. She also made dresses for people. No doubt, she had a hard life. Then James Marlow came along, a kind and nonviolent man. She fell for him and wound up pregnant and unmarried. He did marry her before I was born though. When she was eight months pregnant with me, they walked out of the mountains to Sherwood to get groceries. This was in the days of the steam locomotive trains. There was a water tank in Sherwood, so the trains would stop there and take on water before they started up the mountain. This particular day, it was a passenger train. A pretty woman waved at James Marlow from the train. He told Mom, "I'll see ya later," and he walked over to the train, climbed aboard, and came back when I was eleven months old. Mom ran him off, so I never knew my daddy. By the time I was school-age, Mom had married the third time. He was a good man in many ways. He was a hard worker, yet he didn't know how to make a dollar. Somehow, everyone else seemed to be eating well, except for us, and we went to bed hungry night after night. I think he just let people take advantage of him. I do know one thing for sure though: We were really poor.

Mom was mad at life, probably at herself mostly for the poor decisions she had made. The biggest problem though was me. I was always around (the reminder of her biggest and most shameful mistake). I think she grew to hate me. I never blamed her for it, though. I think when she looked at me, she only saw James Marlow, the man who left her standing by the railroad track, brokenhearted and pregnant. She never saw that little redheaded boy who needed love and affection so badly. I grew to be hard-hearted, just like her. I didn't care if I lived or died. I can't remember when she whipped me without bringing blood. She used to knock me down and sit on my stomach and beat my head into the floor. I never offered to strike back. She was still my mother. As she beat me, she would say, "You James Marlow–looking thing, I'll kill you!" I would just say, "Hit me again. I hope you do kill me!"

The older kids would cry and beg her not to hit me again, but it didn't seem to faze her.

CHAPTER 5

Conditioning

THE MAN MY mom married when I was four, had a little sawmill along with his brother. My stepdad did the work while his brother took care of the books. By the time the mill workers and the bookkeeper got paid, we were lucky to have enough money to buy flour, lard, and cornmeal with. I have seen the time when we had to eat water gravy three times in one day. We didn't have milk to put in it. We couldn't make biscuits without milk. One day, we had thirteen cents, so my stepdad and I headed three miles into town. A loaf of bread cost fourteen cents. We found a penny on the street and got the loaf of bread and headed home to eat our water gravy.

Mom wasn't getting many clothes to wash, but sometimes she would get to clean someone's house. There were two girls still at home, so they took care of the house when Mom got to work. My half brother was usually around, but he didn't like to work. He also had a wife and child, who were supported by her parents. About the only thing he did was fight. He took great pride in beating the biggest man he could find half to death. If he ran out of men to fight, he would slap me around. I was just a kid. He was twenty years older than me. He was always Mom's favorite child though. His excuse for being like he was, was because the world was against him. Mom believed him. Between Mom's beatings and being kicked around by him, I had a hard life. I don't really regret it though. They were just conditioning me for survival in a hard world. I learned to hold my head high and face whatever came my way. Right to this day, I am a survivor. I have someone who holds my hand today though and walks me through the bad times and the good. I know He walked me through those terrible childhood days too. Praise be to the Holy Spirit Who guides me.

I remember one time, when I was about twelve years old, my half brother had been put in jail for something. No one would go post his bail except this one moonshiner. The stipulation was that he would pay him back with three hundred pounds of sugar because sugar was hard to come by. The government was cracking down on illegal whiskey, so they rationed sugar. My brother knew where probably the biggest still in that part of the country was. He made me go with him to this still in the middle of the night and steal their sugar. They must have had enough to fill a trailer truck. With no light and two burlap sacks, we headed up the mountain. I probably didn't weigh eighty pounds. I only weighed 110 when I went in the Navy at age seventeen, so I don't know how he expected me to carry 150 pounds of sugar. The still was just about to the top of the mountain, and it was a hard walk over big limestone rocks and briars as big as your finger. You didn't have a road going to the still either, like they show on TV. This was the real thing. We knew, if we got caught, we would be killed and thrown in a sinkhole on the side of that mountain, never to be seen again. When we got near, we could tell they were working. Their sugar was stacked up under tarps. We sneaked in there and got three hundred pounds without being seen. Sometimes they would walk within three feet of us. If there is one thing I dislike most, it's a thief. And yet I am telling you these things. I was letting someone lead me to do the thing I hate most. My half brother put it in the sacks, and we eased away a foot at a time on our belly until we were finally far enough away to stand up. Needless to say, we hardly got anywhere at all until I tried to get rid of some of mine, but he wouldn't let me. He did take fifty pounds out of my sack and put it into his though. So I had one hundred pounds, and he had two hundred pounds. That sure helped me a lot, but we still had a long way to go. I think I did more falling down the mountain than walking down it. Just before we got to the bottom, he took another 25 pounds. Now he had 225, and I had 75. A man was supposed to pick us up at the foot of the mountain on an old gravel road at a half hour before daylight. Just as we got there, he drove up.

Perfect timing! We threw the sugar in the trunk of his car and took off. Man, was I ever glad to be heading home. I looked like I had been in a hatchet fight. I had blood all over me from the cuts and skinned places from falling all over the limestone rocks, and the big briars had torn gashes in my skin. I think that taught me that crime didn't pay!

The way I was headed though was downhill. Did I have a chance?—I guess about as much chance as a snowball in July.

CHAPTER 6

Fight or Flight—Choosing My Battles...Wisely?

WHEN I WAS a child, I didn't have toys. They were for people who had idle time. I never had a child's life. I got my first gun when I was five years old. I guess I always had a knife also. I was taught how to use them very well. They were for hunting, skinning, and personal protection. I was never supposed to miss with that little single-shot, twenty-two rifle. We couldn't afford to waste the ammo. I don't know how we ever came up with enough ammo for me to even learn how to hit anything. I guess the Lord did the aiming for me.

At daylight, I would be sitting under a hickory tree somewhere in the woods, waiting for a squirrel to come out and get him a nut. *Bang*! My breakfast just fell out of a tree—one shot, one piece of meat.

We couldn't afford a box of shells. They cost a penny a piece. We would go to the store and buy two or three shells at a time. If I went hunting with three shells and came home with one, then I better have two pieces of meat. I remember when I was about ten years old; I was hunting when, all of a sudden, a black bear growled and stood up on its hind legs! I had never seen a bear before, but I knew what it was! I guess I never even thought like a child. I had to decide and fast! I knew my twenty-two was no match for a bear, and if I wounded it, it might charge. I backed away slowly, one step at a time. Once again, I walked away with my life. Thanks again, Lord.

At this time of my life, we lived a mile off the highway up in a hollow. I would walk to the road every morning and catch the school bus. It was only two miles then to school. My heart was growing harder all the time, and I didn't care about anything or anybody. No one needed me, and I sure didn't need anybody.

I got in a fight on the school bus when I was in the seventh grade, so the school bus driver made me sit on the front row so he could watch me. My seat was the right rear, normally. One morning, I didn't want to go to school, but Mom kicked my rear end and made me go. I was mad and felt like taking it out on someone. Why not the bus driver? I decided I had ridden in the front seat my last time. As I started to go by the driver; he grabbed me. We had it out. As I said before, I was not riding the front seat again. I guess I showed him! Now I couldn't ride the bus. Period! I walked that mile back home just to get my fanny kicked right up around my neck. Now I had to walk three miles every morning and three miles every evening.

Mom made sure I got off to school each morning. It was winter, and the kids looked so warm as they passed by on that bus for three months. Finally, my older sister begged the bus driver until he agreed to let me ride again, but only on the front seat. My pride sure was hurt, but at least it was warm. Shortly after that, the principal and I had a disagreement, and I took him on. I lost that one also. I got expelled. The next year, I repeated the seventh grade and then finally passed to the eighth.

CHAPTER 7

A Taste of Wealth

THERE WAS A man who hired a contractor to put asphalt shingles on the sides of his two-story house when I was thirteen years old, and I got a job helping him for one dollar a day. The shingles were very heavy, and I carried them up the scaffold so he could install them. You can believe me, I earned that dollar a day! It took us seven days to complete the job. He paid me off with seven crisp one-dollar bills.

My mom made my shirts out of sacks that flour and horse feed came in. We always had plenty of them because my stepdad always had either horses or mules so we could pull the logs to the sawmill. Mom also made my winter coats from whatever material she could find. My shoes came from a secondhand store in the valley. They were worse when we bought them than the ones, I throw away today. Most of the time, when we got them, the soles were loose and floppy. We would take them home and take wire and wire the soles on. I took my seven dollars and walked into town and went to the general store. I bought myself the best pair of high-top shoes they had for $6.50, a belt for $0.25, and still had enough left for some candy and bubble gum! Boy! Was I ever proud of myself!

This certainly wasn't the first time I worked, just the first time I didn't have to help buy groceries. My stepdad put me to carrying water to the mill hands from a spring up the hill when I was four when he married Mom. I carried a pint at a time. I would fall three or four times a day and break the jar, but they kept plenty of extras for me. I graduated from that to snaking logs when I was six. This was when timber was cut by two men pulling a crosscut saw. I guess most people nowadays don't know what they were used for. They weren't always used to hang on the wall in a rustic retreat cabin. The timber cutters would drive the grabs in the logs for me, and I would hook the horses up and drag the logs to the mill. One of the mill hands, called the off foreman, would knock the grabs off the logs, and I would hang them on the harness and then ride the horse back to get another one.

    Each fall, I always had to pick cotton. It wasn't done by machines in those days. We even got out of school two weeks each fall for cotton-picking. Today, kids get out of school for fall break so they can sleep half the day and play video games the rest of the day. I would like every child to have to pick cotton one season. They would find out what real work is and appreciate what they have. They would really appreciate what they have if they had to work and earn money to help pay for their groceries.

CHAPTER 8

Visitors

I GUESS I was never a child really. I went from an infant to manhood. It was such a struggle just to survive. We didn't have electricity or running water. To this day, when I turn the light switch on or the faucet on, I think of how fortunate I am. My house is so wonderfully warm in the winter and cool in the summer, all with a touch of a switch.

As a kid, we didn't have floor coverings. We just had old, rough boards, but Mom scrubbed them until they were spotless all the time. She was a very clean housekeeper. She was also one who wouldn't let any animal inside her house except one that had been killed, skinned, and ready to cook.

I remember one time, one of the few times someone could drive a car up to the house, we looked out, and there came a nice shinny car; a Hudson it was. When they started getting out, Mom said, "That's uncle so and so." I don't recall what the name was. My older sister happened to be there, and she noticed they had a little Chihuahua dog. They were called asthma dogs in those days. Supposedly, they helped people to breathe better or something to that effect. With Mom, it didn't make any difference what it was used for. Its place was under the front porch. The cat's place was in the barn. My sister had to appeal to her and fast! "Mom, they have a little dog that can't live outside. It has to be inside." Mom was really nice about it. They came in, and she never said a word, but she kept one eye on that dog at all times. If it had raised its hind leg for any reason, I guarantee it would have been squashed like a roach bug by Mom's foot. It was getting late in the day, so Mom got up from her chair and went to the back bedroom and then came back and said, "I have changed the sheets on the bed and lit the lamp for you guys, so when you want to go to bed, feel free to do so. Oh, and I have put some clean rags in a box and put them next to the door on the back porch for your little dog so it will be warm.

They looked at her and said, "Our dog sleeps with us!"

She said, "Not in my bed."

They said, "If our dog can't sleep there, neither can we."

She said, "Like I said, no dog sleeps in my bed."

End of conversation.

They got up, took their dog and suitcase, and down the road they went, never to be heard from again. Mom said they lived in Detroit, Michigan.

CHAPTER 9

Fire on the Mountain

SOON WE MOVED again—this time, farther from town, ten miles from the nearest house or highway, way back in the mountains. Now it was just my mom, stepdad, and me. The two girls had left home by then.

My stepdad came up with an old junker of a car that he got somewhere. His job was to look for forest fires from a hundred-foot tower. There was a gasoline engine, which pulled a generator. It would make just enough electricity to power the radio and one light bulb if he spotted a fire. He would crank up the old car and take me to the foot of the mountain each morning, then pick me up at the same place each afternoon. I would catch the school bus there each day. We would leave home way before daylight and usually get stuck at least once and have to jack the old car up and hunt rocks to put under the rear wheels to get out of a mudhole. I would get out of my old muddy clothes and put clean ones on before the bus came. That afternoon, I would get back in the car and put my old muddy clothes back on, and away we would go again.

I would get home way after dark and have to get my homework done by the light of a kerosene lamp. I would try to get him to start the generator to give me light, but he would say no. That generator was to power the radio in the tower in case of a fire, and it would be cheating to use it for anything else.

CHAPTER 10

Winter Woes

I MANAGED TO go to school in the fall, or at least most of the time. When the winter freeze would come, we managed fine as long as the ground was frozen. The problem was the spring thaw. There was no getting off the mountain then, so I would have to quit school. I did this three years in a row when I was in the eighth grade, so I have gone through life with a seventh-grade formal education. I don't think it held me back that much though. I can do all things through Jesus Christ who strengthens me.

Those days were rough though out there on that mountain. The old house was just an outer shell with no insulation or inner walls. It would snow at night, and our beds would be white the next morning where the snow would blow through the cracks. At night, we would put the irons that Mom used to press our clothes, on the stove, and get them hot and then put them under the covers at the foot of the bed to keep from freezing. We would let the fire go out at night to preserve wood. The next morning, we would get up and get the heating stove going and then go to the kitchen and get the cookstove going. We would put the water bucket, which had the water dipper in it, on the stove to thaw. While it was thawing, we would take turns going to the outhouse. That was one trip you didn't take until you absolutely had to. Mom would usually go first so she could get back in and get washed up and start breakfast. She would fix whatever we had on hand at the time. It all depended on what we could kill or if we had enough money to buy groceries. A new day dawning for the same old routine!

Each Saturday and Sunday, we spent cutting wood for the following week.

CHAPTER 11

Replenishing

THE STATE HAD just stocked the mountain with deer, and they would come up to the house. I tried to get my stepdad to let me kill one so we would have meat to eat. He said, "No. They put the deer here to be protected for ten years. If they don't allow anyone to hunt them for that period of time, there will be fine hunting someday. If everyone decided to shoot just one, the deer population would never get started."

He was right. There is an abundance of deer in these mountains today. People today can't imagine the temptation we faced when our stomach was growling from emptiness. It was hard to choose right from wrong.

I guess that must have been about the time when game laws were made or at least started to be enforced. To this day, I respect all game laws and only hunt in season. I also hunt only what I intend to eat. I was taught some good things, yet I was taught a lot of bad things. I was confused. Thank God I never forgot the good things. I've tried so hard to forget the bad things, but it's hard to erase them completely from my mind. I do know one thing for certain though: the Holy Spirit leads and guides me every step of the way.

CHAPTER 12

The Calling

ONE SUMMER SUNDAY morning, when I didn't have to cut wood, I walked off that mountain. When I got to the main highway, I hitchhiked to Decherd. It's a small town where one of my sisters lived with her husband and children. They took me to church with them. When the altar call came, I headed down that aisle. I really didn't know what I was doing. Oh, I knew there was God in heaven, but I didn't fully understand anything about Him. You know, all these many years later, I'm sort of still in that same boat. How much do we really know about God?

The one thing which is most important is, I know what faith is and that I can put all my faith in God. I've tried it and can give you firsthand knowledge. We can talk more on that subject later. Now back to the day I walked that aisle. My knees were weak, and my hands were trembling. I walked, but where was I going and why? I knew God was calling me, but to do what? I guess you have figured out by now that I was brought up in anything but a Christian home. I was taught how to hurt, not how to love. I needed someone to teach me, and I didn't get that at home. There was a Bible in the house, but I was not allowed to read it. It was there because it had important information in it, like everybody in the family's name and birthday. Those, I found out later in life, were the least important words in the whole book. I wish someone at that church would have given me my own Bible.

God knew I was in for a long, hard journey, and He never gave up on me. I know He has been disappointed in me and even ashamed of me, but He never turned His back on me.

I couldn't walk off that mountain and back every weekend to go to church, so I never learned how a Christian was supposed to act, but I do know the Holy Spirit talked to me from that day on. So did Satan. It was like someone on each shoulder. One was more aggressive than the other. He would tell me, "Go ahead and do it. It will be fun." The other voice would softly say, "You will be sorry!" I would listen to the first voice and go ahead and do it…and then I was sorry that I did! Someday I would learn what the Holy Spirit was. Thank You, Lord, for being so tolerant. I am so sorry it took me so long to give my soul to You. I know now You had already claimed it. You were waiting for the right time, a time when I would voluntarily turn my life over to You. You wanted 100 percent, not 10 percent or 20 percent or whatever.

CHAPTER 13

From a Boy to a Man

WHEN I WAS fifteen years old, we moved off the mountain. For the next couple of years, I had several jobs. One was mixing mud for a mason to lay bricks. Another was driving a dump truck and hauling coal from the mines to people's homes in town.

Then I got sick and had to go to the hospital. I don't really know what was wrong with me, but I went to work for the doctor who also owned the hospital in Tullahoma. Dr. King was his name. I farmed for him for $20 a week. I paid $10 a week on my hospital bill and $5 a week for my room and board with a family who took me in. That left me $5 a week. And if I went home on the weekend, it took half of that for bus fare. It was rough, but it kept me out of trouble.

Two years passed, and I turned seventeen in November and went to the first military recruiter I came to. It happened to be the Navy. Mom signed the papers to enlist me. They paid my bus fare to go to Nashville for my exam. No one thought I would make it because of only having a seventh grade education. It turned out that my size was the problem. You had to weigh at least 115 pounds. I weighed 109 pounds. They sent me back home for a couple of weeks so that I could try to gain six pounds. I returned two weeks later and stepped on the scales. They still read 109. They told me to go to the water fountain and drink water until my eyeballs floated. I did and once again stepped on the scales. They still read 109. They told me to eat bananas the next morning until they ran out of my ears. I did, and the scales still read 109. The guy scratched his head and said, "This is impossible!" I proved him wrong. He asked me how bad did I want to go into the military? I said, "Bad." So he jacked my weight up on paper and snuck me through. I was sworn in on the twenty-sixth day of December and shipped out on the next plane to San Diego, California, for boot camp.

In those days, boot camp was rough. There were seventy-five guys in my company, and ten weeks later, there were twenty-five. Several of them tried to commit suicide. I was the least likely one to make it, but I did. After boot camp, I was sent to an aircraft squadron in Norfolk, Virginia. I'll never forget the night I arrived.

From the airport, I had to catch a bus to the base. Along came a bus that read on the front of it "Navy Base." It took me to the ship docks. I was supposed to catch the bus that said, "Naval Air Station." It was several miles across the base. Not knowing what to do, I started following any sign that read naval air station, and with a complete seabag on my back, I walked all the way across the biggest naval installation in the U.S!

Stupidity was never in me, but I sure was eaten up with ignorance!

CHAPTER 14

Ignorance

SPEAKING OF IGNORANCE, I remember when I went to Nashville to join the military. They put me up in a hotel. I believe it was the Noelle Hotel. I wouldn't have left that hotel for anything! I had never been to a big city like that before, and I was afraid I would get lost. In the room, there was a radio hanging on the wall. I turned the knob. It clicked, and in a few seconds, music started playing! I turned the knob to the left. It clicked and turned off—simple enough. I got this.

In the corner of the room was a television. I believe I'll check that out. I had seen televisions before, but I had never operated one before. It said above the knob, "Off, on, volume." I turned the knob to the right…nothing. I turned the knob to the left…nothing. I looked behind it, and it was plugged into the wall. See, I wasn't stupid. I knew it had to be plugged in. I messed with that thing till 1:00 a.m. and never got anything out of it. I decided it was broken, so I went to bed.

When I got to my duty station in Norfolk, Virginia, there was a TV lounge. One evening, I went in there and looked around. There was a TV in there, like the one in Nashville—same thing. I sat down and started reading a book. In a few minutes, a guy came in, walked over to the TV, pulled out on that knob, and a picture was on the screen! LIB, that's Southern for "Well, I'll be! What about that?" They didn't say pull the knob. I would never have pulled on it. Another plus for my mom was that she always taught me to respect other people's property. What if I had pulled on that knob and it fell off? I wouldn't have been able to sleep that night!

CHAPTER 15

Getting My Wings

I HAD A lot to learn and fast. I started hitting the books and learning as much about airplanes as possible. I started watching the older more seasoned men over their shoulders, and then I would go to the books to find out why they did the things they did. No one would give me the time of day. One day, this guy came out to start up a plane to check it out. I asked if I could start it. Of course, he outranked me by many stripes and about twenty-five years. He laughed at me and said, "Do you think I'm crazy? You would blow it sky high!"

I was about like a little banty rooster with a short fuse. I had to stand on my tip toes to see his chin, and of course I showed my fanny. I told him I could start the thing as good as him or anyone else. It is a wonder he didn't have me court-martialed, but he didn't. He just calmly looked down at me and said, "You really believe that, don't you?"

I said, "I don't just believe it, I know it!"

He said, "Get in there and show me."

So I climbed into the cockpit and got perfect starts on both reciprocating engines!

He wanted to know how I knew how to do it, and I told him how I had been looking over the shoulders of men like him and then hitting the books to see why they did the things they did. From that day on, he took me under his wing and taught me everything. He also taught me how to start the two jet engines, which were on the plane. Within six months, I was flying the position of plane captain. As far as I know, I was the youngest man to fly that position. I pushed throttles. I had to know how much time we had left on our fuel at all times, which depended on our power settings and the altitude we were flying at. I had to know what we always weighed, which depended on how much fuel we had burned and how much ordinance we had dropped and, once again, our altitude. It was a very important position and a lot to learn for an old country boy with a seventh-grade education. I was proud of how far I had come in such a short length of time.

I know where this knowledge came from. The Lord was blessing me, although I was not living the life He called me to live. The life I was living was the life of a lost person. God was so patient with me. I can't possibly comprehend His love and patience. He had work for me in the future, but that was a long way down the road.

CHAPTER 16

The Nut Doesn't Fall Far from the Tree

IN THE MEANTIME, I was a drunkard, as well as anything else you might want to call me. My daddy was known for good booze, fancy clothes, and pretty women. What the heck, everybody always said I was just like him. I might as well live up to the name. I never knew him, yet I was walking in his footsteps.

I believe right to this day that you can speak evil on someone and cause them harm. It was spoken on me until I thought I had no control of my life. I was destined to live the life of James Marlow, not Jimmy Marlow. It took years before I cast all that behind me, which I will discuss later.

CHAPTER 17

Deployment

FOR FOUR YEARS we were on the move, chasing Russian submarines all over the Atlantic Ocean. Some of the places we went to were nice, and some were the pits. Some of the places we went to did not have any facilities for us, and we slept on the ground and wrapped up in a blanket at night.

The food we had to eat was nonperishable: sardines, peanut butter, Beanie Weenies, and crackers and things like that.

When the Cuban Crisis started, we were there. You don't hear much about things like that anymore. Fidel Castro let the Russians come in there to set up missile sites. The US owned one corner of the island called Guantanamo Bay. We set up a blockade and turned the Russians' back.

I was there when Castro gave us twenty-four hours to leave. He said the first shot he fired, he would come through the gate, and the second shot, he would be eating in our mess hall. President John F. Kennedy told him, "You might fire one shot, but you will never fire another!" The rest of that story is history. Fifty or so years later, and we still own Guantanamo Bay, and the Russians still have no missile sites in Cuba.

Iceland is a neutral country, and the Russians would always go there. Where they went, we followed. I was there four different times. I have been there when it was dark twenty-four hours a day, and I have been there in the middle of summer when it was daylight twenty-four hours a day. I never figured how those people coped with that, but I believe they were some of the proudest people I ever saw.

CHAPTER 18

Join the Military, See the World

WE WENT TO many other places, some good and some not so good. I remember one place where we went was Souda Bay, Crete. From what I gather today, it is a well sought-after island, with expensive homes and beautiful beaches. When I was there, it wasn't like that. This was the place where we had no facilities. On the other end of the island, it was nice, so I and two of my buddies got a pass to go there for a couple of days. We drank a lot in those days, so you might imagine what it was going to be like. It was an eight-hour bus ride. We got to see a lot of the countryside. A lot of people lived in grass huts, and the roads were rough and narrow.

When we got to where we were going, which I don't even remember the name of the place, I went out and rented a car. How?—I don't know because no one spoke English, and I sure couldn't speak Greek. I rented a VW Beetle. We went to some beach and wound up finding two guys who were hitchhiking around the world. They were the only people we found who could speak English. One was from Ireland, and one was from Scotland. We managed to cram five people into that bug, and it was like sardines in a can. Down the road we went, and wouldn't you know it? I ran off the road about twenty feet straight down. I don't know how many times we rolled, but when we stopped, we were lying on the right side. Once again, the Lord had to have put a hedge of angels around us because none of us were hurt. I pushed the driver's door open, and we managed to crawl out. The car was torn all to pieces. We all got against the car and pushed it over on its wheels. I tried the starter, and it started. We got back in and took off through this field, trying to find a place to get back on the road. At one point, we came to a place where there was a fence post and a utility pole. We decided that the space was about a foot too narrow. What the heck, the car is already totaled. All the fenders were bent up anyway, so if we leave a couple in the field, it wouldn't matter. We made it back to the road. We could only travel about ten miles per hour, but the little bug got us back to the hotel.

The next morning, at the crack of dawn, it sounded like someone was knocking my door down. It was the Greek police and the man I rented the car from. It turned out he could say a few words in English. I don't know all of what he was saying, but he did manage to get one thing across, that he would kill me before I got off the island!

They put me in jail. That is a weird feeling when you are in jail in a foreign country, and no one speaks your language, and you can't speak theirs. It turned out, the man who rented me the car was a communist, and they didn't care for his kind. (A huge plus in my favor!) He had rented me his personal car for one day. I thought I had rented it for as long as I wanted it from an agency. Wrong! I was supposed to have it back before sundown. The Greek authorities went to an air force base, which happened to be somewhere near, and got an interpreter. Boy, what a relief!! They had a hearing right away. I was released with the promise that I would return in twenty-four hours with $500. The price of a new VW was about $1,500.

I went back to the other end of the island where my squadron was, which took eight hours. I borrowed from about every man in the whole outfit, and I got the $500. I believe, the most I got from any one individual was $20! Some gave $10, some gave $5, and some gave $2 and $3. I was broke for a long time until I got everyone paid back. I only made about $200 a month, and that was including my $50 a month extra for being on a flight crew. The shore patrol took me and the money back, so that saved a little time. The jeep was faster than the bus. When I paid the money back, they gave me a release form, printed in Greek on one side and English on the other side. It read, "The Greek government does not hold the US responsible for the wrongdoing of Jimmy O. Marlow." (Could it be the Lord was trying to get my attention?) Not yet, Lord!

I think back, and chills run up my spine even now. How undeserving I was and am. How forgiving and long-suffering the Lord has been. I wish I still had that release form. I took it to my mom's house, and I think my brother threw it away, along with everything else of mine that he could find.

Puerto Rico

I remember, one time in Puerto Rico, I was in an establishment, drinking with my friends. Some local fellow came in and wanted us Americans to come outside so he could kill us simply because he didn't like Americans. He was waving a pistol around, and the owner of the establishment said it wasn't legal for him to kill us inside, but it was all right if we were outside. It sounded crazy, but he meant business. So we sat inside, laughing about it while he waited outside. He seemed pretty intent on waiting us out, so I decided to do something about it.

I sneaked out the back door, only to find a ten-foot-high fence around the backyard, with no way out. It was made of roofing tin. I found the perfect escape route. Just so happened, there was a big tree in the yard with a limb that hung over the fence. I climbed it, went over the fence, and dropped down into the next yard, which turned out to be fenced in also! This one was just a normal high fence. Wouldn't you know it? There was a big dog that came after me!

I had no trouble clearing that fence whatsoever. I walked the streets until I found a police station. There was one man there. I told him my story, and he told me there was nothing he could do about it. He said someone would be in to help him in a few hours, and he would come and check out the situation. Now here I was, outside, while my friends were still inside. I wasn't going to leave them there, but there wasn't much I could do. I had no weapon and no way of getting one, so I decided to go back the way I had come.

I got back to where the dog was, and he seemed to be asleep. I sneaked back across the yard. I didn't know if I could jump high enough to reach that limb or not, but I had to try. I could barely jump high enough, but I made it. I got back over to the other yard and went back in with my friends. We waited, and so did that guy. We finally figured, after a couple hours, we had no choice but to rush him since it was almost daylight. Finally, he got in his car and drove away! Thank You, Lord, once again. We didn't hurt the guy, and he didn't hurt us. We didn't even think of how serious that could have been. We just thought it was funny. When would I ever learn?

I take no pride in telling these things. It makes me heavyhearted just thinking about them, and I would like to leave them out, but I can't. I tell you these things, hoping somewhere, some young man will read these words and understand he is going down a one-way street in the wrong direction and turnaround. The Lord has been overly tolerant with me. The next young man may not be so fortunate.

I would eventually turn my life over to him…but not yet.

CHAPTER 19

Be All You Can Be

GOD USES CHRISTIANS to show how the lost should live and make the lost want what they have. I don't mean just a churchgoer. There are people sitting on the front row in church houses every Sunday who will have a front seat in hell. I am talking about people who will walk the walk of a Christian. Walking the walk isn't always easy or popular. I am talking about Christians who will talk the talk—someone who will stand solid for God in the midst of a sinful world, someone who is brave enough to stand up for what is right and godly when your opponents outnumber you twenty to one, someone who reads their Bible and will teach it at the drop of a hat. People must see things in order to be led by them. You can't be led by words alone. So you so-called Christians out there, straighten up and let the world see what a Christian is supposed to act like.

I'm getting a little ahead of myself. At that particular time in my life, I wasn't living like a Christian myself, but I will be as soon as I find someone to lead me and teach me.

Until then, I must go through and learn a lot more lessons during my wicked life.

Many other things happened to me, and as I look back, I see where God protected me. He must have cried a lot when he looked down on me. I continued to fly all over, and it seemed we had some kind of emergency about every time we got off the ground. We never thought anything about it though. That was just part of our job. Remember that, folks, when you see a military person. He or she must be willing to risk their lives at all times.

I don't speak more highly for one branch of the armed forces or the other or for one's position as opposed to another. It takes every man and woman in each branch to do what must be done.

I remember, on one mission, we flew for ten hours one night right in the middle of a hurricane. We were looking for something off a spaceship the size of a softball. That was one bad night. I remember a couple other times when we almost got blown out of the air. Make that three times—no, four times! Well, it only takes once anyway. Thank You, Lord, that it never happened. I remember flying through the Bermuda Triangle many times. We did have a few times when something minor happened. Once, all communications were lost. Another time, an engine caught fire. And then an antenna that went from the top of the vertical stabilizer to the center of the fuselage, which we called the clothesline, broke. We always made it back safely though, except for the night that I was on a night patrol.

CHAPTER 20

Mistaken Identity

I HAD BEEN out on a night flight and came in about daylight and went to bed. About the time when I got to sleeping well, the master-at-arms of the barracks came and woke me up and said the Red Cross wanted to talk to me on the phone. When I answered, they said, "How do you feel?"

I said, "Fine, except tired from being on patrol all night."

They said, "Are you not hurt?"

I replied, "No! I am not. What's going on?"

They said, "Call home. Someone in the Red Cross has already called or is in the process of calling and telling your family that your plane went down at sea, and you are missing."

I said, "How did this happen? I was on patrol, but we did not crash."

They said, "Your name is Jimmy Marlow?"

"Yes."

"You are in VP-24?"

"Yes."

"Your rank is so and so?"

"Yes."

"Your service number is so and so, right?"

"Wrong."

It turned out the guy's name was Jimmy Marrow, and he was in VS-24. I called home and talked to my mom. She said she had not received a call from the Red Cross yet. I told her, if she did, that it was a mistake. I met this Jimmy Marrow a year later. He was not killed in the crash. He did not fly again though. I do not remember how many were killed, but he survived. One other time, my crew and another crew from our sister squadron went out on patrol together and were coming in at the same time. We circled the field and let the other plane land first. It crashed and burned on the runway. We had to use another runway to land. My friends thought it was my plane and were sad but rejoiced when I walked in.

CHAPTER 21

Countdown

THERE WERE SO many other times I could have been killed but wasn't. I finally got near to the end of my four-year hitch and was counting the days to when I could finally go home, and then Vietnam started getting hot, so they extended my hitch for six more months. I think I was in Rome, Italy, when I got the news. I never set foot on Vietnam soil. We did patrol places where Russian subs might cross on their way to Vietnam though.

When we got back to Norfolk, Virginia, I was counting the days again. One evening, about dark, another plane captain went out and started a plane up to check it out. He must not have pulled a proper preflight inspection on the plane before he started it up, and it caught on fire. I don't know where he went after that; all I know is that he left! I don't know why I went to the plane, but I did. I climbed up in the cockpit without even thinking about it until I realized I was sitting in the pilot's seat. There was a fire so hot coming from one of the jets that it melted. There was four thousand gallons of fuel in the wings also. The only way to put a fire like that out is to starve it. There were proper procedures to follow, and I knew them well. I got the fire out, but people thought I was the one who started the plane, so naturally, they thought I would be court-martialed and go to the brig.

The one who started the plane only had a very few days left before his honorable discharge, and I wasn't going to squeal on him. A few days after his discharge, a message came over the loudspeaker: "Marlow, report to the captain's office immediately." As I walked to the captain's office, passing several of the other men on the way, all I could hear was them saying that they would visit me in the brig.

When I entered the skipper's office, the executive officer was there also. They told me to be at ease. They didn't ask me any questions at all. The skipper said, "Marlow, we have been doing some research and have come to the conclusion that not only did you save a multimillion-dollar aircraft for the Navy, but possibly many lives as well! We congratulate you on a job well done."

When everyone heard the news, I was their hero then! Before he knew the truth, the maintenance officer, who was the third man in charge, told me that I was going to be hung from the highest yardarm. When he heard the truth, he came up to me and put his arm on my shoulder and started to praise me, which made me mad! I told him, "Do not touch me, sir! You never asked me what happened. You just wanted to hang me, so keep your hands off of me, sir!" He turned and walked away. Shortly after that, my time was up, and I took my honorable discharge and headed to Tennessee.

CHAPTER 22

Civilian Life

THE NEXT PHASE of my life was a lot different in one way and about the same in another. I had to do a lot of adjusting to civilian life, yet I was still as rotten as before. There weren't any jobs to speak of around home, so I decided to go North.

Up there, if you didn't like what you were doing, you could quit and go across the street and go to work doing something else. I tried most of them. I was never afraid of hard work. I just got bored easily. I tried Ford Motor Company as a line worker in the stamping plant. I didn't like that. I tried assembly line work at the engine assembly plant at Allis-Chalmers. I didn't like that. They recognized my work in the Navy when I wasn't flying, so I went to work in their machine shop as a machinist. I did well at everything I did but couldn't seem to find something I enjoyed.

I know most people wouldn't agree with my way of thinking, but money is not what it is all about. Satisfaction and contentment are what matters. I have seen people go to work for thirty years hating that job from the first day, still hating it the day they retire. They wind up grumpy, old, rich men. I always said I wouldn't live my life like that. That is not living. It is existing and nothing more.

I tried truck driving, being a salesperson, a railroad worker, and even worked in the oil fields. I was still looking. I always made good money and had a good name everywhere I went. I tried being a carpenter, which I enjoyed most until I learned how to run heavy equipment.

Was there something else that I was looking for though? Maybe it wasn't the jobs at all? Could it be time to yield to the call of the Lord?

Not yet, Lord.

CHAPTER 23

Close Call

ONE DAY, I was helping my brother and brother-in-law work on their cars in a garage. We had the door open, and we started one of the cars up for about ten minutes and shut it off. A few minutes later, my brother just fell in the floor. I tried to stuff him in the back seat of a two-door car, afraid my sister would come out there and find him drunk and passed out. He wasn't even drinking though. I could not get him in the car, so I just threw him down on the concrete. I looked over at my brother-in-law, who was leaning against the wall, and said, "The heck with him. You can't freeze a drunk." My brother-in-law slid down the wall, looked up at me, and said, "Dang, Jim, I believe I'm drunk too. You bunch of drunks get me in here to work on your cars, and then both of you pass out on me."

None of us had been drinking. My mind was fading, too, but I didn't realize it. I don't know how much time passed. My sister had just started smoking and ran out of cigarettes. She came out to the garage to get a cigarette from us. She found all of us lying on the floor. She called the fire department, and they took the other two to the hospital. I really don't know the whole story with me. All I know is when I came to, I was in the hospital but later had to go to the funeral home to pay my bill. Apparently, they thought I was dead, so they took me to the funeral home before they realized I wasn't dead. So they then took me to the hospital. I survived, though!

When they found out I was alive, they said I would have brain damage. If I do, no one knows. The only thing I have noticed is that I forget certain things easily, such as being introduced to someone and forgetting their name by the time I get through shaking their hand. I have written about thirty songs, yet I cannot remember the words to any of them unless I have the paper in front of me. I have led the music in church for years and wouldn't attempt to sing "Amazing Grace" without the words in front of me.

One thing I learned from this is, it's true; you can't smell or taste carbon monoxide. You just go to sleep.

Lord, just kill me. I don't deserve to live. Why and how are You so tolerant? Someday I will understand, and it will make me a better human being. The doctor said, the outside air was so cold, it drove those fumes right into our lungs and collapsed them. All three of us survived. Thank You, Lord.

CHAPTER 24

Snowstorm of Love

MORE CHANGES ARE about to come. It was winter in Chicagoland. A snowstorm slipped right through the radar. I was working in a machine shop about a dozen blocks from where I lived with my sister and brother-in-law and their two small children. There was no forecast for snow, yet it started coming a blizzard at 11:00 a.m. Everyone wanted to go home, but the management said, "No!" At 3:00 p.m., they were running us out of the plant.

The plant had a flat roof, and they were afraid that if the snow built up on it, then it would collapse. You could only see about half of the windshield on the cars in the parking lots, and the wind must have been gale force. Other people were flocking to the bars, restaurants, and stores with no other places to go. They lived in those places for the next few days until they could be rescued by snowmobiles.

I managed to get home by walking through the snow above my waist. About a block away from where I lived was a tiny factory. This little girl came out of the factory entrance, wearing gym shoes and a thin jacket. She said she couldn't get home, so she was going to try to make it to her uncle's house, which was entirely too far to walk. I, being the Southern gentleman that I am, helped her down the street. When we got to my house, I told her she should come in and warm up before going any farther. She was not having any part of that. She said, "Oh, no. I am not going in there with you!"

I said, "Look, lady, I am not going to bother you. I don't live here alone. I live with my sister and brother-in-law and their two small children. And if you don't come inside to warm up, you will freeze!"

After arguing a little while more, she finally got cold enough that she agreed. When we got inside, my sister told her there was no way she could make it to her uncle's house. My sister called her mother and explained who she was and that she would take good care of her daughter, and they could talk to each other on the phone. It turned out, both my sister and her mother had heard of each other through some mutual friends. She was a real nice girl, and over the course of three days, we became friends. My sister was a little skinny thing too, so she let her use some of her clothes.

When the storm let up enough, three days later, my brother-in-law and I managed to get her home. We kept in touch after that and sometime later started dating. We dated for about nine or ten months, and then we got married. I don't know why she was attracted to me, or me to her. She was a real Miss Goody Two-shoes, and I was whatever one might want to call me: a womanizer, ladies' man, probably a lot of other things. Everyone said I couldn't be caught, but she caught me. I was finally in love!

I remember when we decided to get married. We rented a cute little furnished apartment, and we would get off work each day and meet at the apartment and work for about two hours a day, painting and fixing it up, just like we wanted it. We both looked forward to each day. We made that place like a dollhouse. *What in the world is happening to me?* I thought. *I am doing things I never thought I would do and, on top of that, enjoying every minute of it!*

We agreed that we would not live with someone else. When we got the little place just like we wanted it, we would get married and spend our wedding night in our own home—such a feeling of accomplishment! Over a half century later, we are still happily married. We both aged a lot, put on a few extra pounds, and picked up a lot of wrinkles along the way, but I think she is prettier now than the day I married her.

CHAPTER 25

What Is Love? (A Little Free Advice)

I CERTAINLY LOVE her more today than the day I married her. When we got married, I didn't know what love was, really. Youngsters tell me all the time, "We're in love," and I tell them, "You don't have the faintest idea of what true love is about." I always ask each one of them, "Are you willing to give 100 percent and expect nothing in return?" If both partners can't honestly say that, then they are not ready for marriage.

Another thing I ask them is, "Are you friends?" Friendship is just as important as love in a marriage. Without friendship, you won't have but one other thing to hold that marriage together. Sex will not keep a marriage together. That's like building a brick home without mortar. Those bricks will look good stacked on top of each other, but the first hint of turbulence, and it will fall to pieces.

I counseled a couple a few years ago who had been married before. At one of the sessions, they told me they wanted a marriage like mine. I told them they couldn't have one like ours. These people were sixty years old! We have been working on our marriage for fifty years to make it what it is. They don't have that much time.

Just a little reality, marriage is like preaching. You don't give up and quit and you don't retire. I am not talking about pastors either. We are all ministers of the gospel if we are Christians.

PART 2

From a Pauper to a Child of the King

CHAPTER 26

Back in Church...Sort Of

AFTER A COUPLE of years of marriage, we decided to get back in church. The first one we went to didn't seem to do anything to make us want to join. The Holy Spirit didn't seem to be present. We tried another, and the preacher didn't seem to preach on anything but tithing. Things just didn't work out, so we drifted away for two or three more years.

We wanted children, but we weren't having any luck at pregnancy. My wife started having a lot of trouble. She started to hemorrhage a lot, and they had to give her a lot of blood. The doctor called us in one day and set us down and said, "If she didn't have a complete hysterectomy, she would die." We wanted children so bad! He set the operation up for thirty days from that visit. As we opened the door, with tears in our eyes about to leave, he said, "There is a higher power that you might try praying to."

That hadn't even entered our minds. Would God hear a prayer from someone who wasn't even in church? In thirty days, not only was she healed, but she was pregnant! The doctor said her due date was March 13, on a Friday. She gave birth to a baby girl on March 14, on a Saturday, at four ten in the morning, eight pounds, three ounces. That no doubt was the happiest day of our lives! We later had another daughter, Eight pounds, three ounces; and then later on a son, eight pounds, eleven ounces!

God, You have proven Your greatness! How could I have been so stupid for so many years? I am Yours, Lord. Take me and use me in whatever way you wish.

My oldest child was nine years old when my wife looked at me and said, "We need to get these children in church." I agreed. The very next Sunday, we went to Sunday school and church. I never looked back. I was finally where God wanted me.

CHAPTER 27

Studying for the Tests

I WANTED TO know all there was about God. I got myself a Bible and started reading in Genesis and didn't stop until I finished Revelation. I then looked back in review and decided I didn't even know what I had just read. I did it again and knew very, very little about the Bible. I did this ten times! I should have it memorized by now, but still very little did I know. I figured I must have written the book on stupidity. I finally heard someone say, you have to study the Bible. Suddenly, I realized I wasn't stupid but ignorant. From that day forward, I have been studying. There is a lot of difference between studying and just reading. After over forty years, I still know so little, but I am trying, and I realize I won't know it all till I get to heaven. I find that book to be the most interesting book I have ever read. It never gets old or out of date, and I never quit learning. I constantly have things to jump out at me that I have overlooked for years! I will tell anyone that might be thinking about taking up reading, the Bible is the book to choose. I do encourage everyone who opens it though to ask God to give them an open heart and mind and a spirit of learning. If you do this, the Holy Spirit will show you amazing things. Only through Him can you understand what you are reading.

Why was I not raised in a Christian home? Maybe it was so I could go through so much unnecessary grief.

When I look back, I see the mistakes I made more than the ones my parents made. Most of the choices I have made in life were my own, not my parents'. So if there is someone out there using that line as an excuse, don't! It won't work. You know who God is, and you know the handbook of life is within your reach.

Been there, bought the T-shirt. When I look back at my past, I hate what I see. It makes me sick. Thank You, Lord, for being so long-suffering. Lord, I will do anything You choose for me to do.

Mistakes still come so easy. With those mistakes, I try to turn them into a learning tool. One mistake I made was trying to get the Lord to wait on me, instead of waiting on the Lord. He waited on me for years. Now I have learned to wait on Him. When one tries to get ahead of God, that means he is going alone. Even though his intentions are good, he is going without the Lord. On the other hand, when God speaks, be ready to act, or you might just regret it.

CHAPTER 28

Family or Fame?

I HAD A shot at being famous but was faced with a choice, one I have never regretted. I have messed around with a guitar most of my adult life. I had written a few country and Western songs. A record company came to town, looking for talent. Several people tried to get me to take some of my songs and try to sell them.

I made an appointment. They told me to bring my guitar so I could sing them. I took a couple of my songs down and sang them. They asked me why I came as a songwriter. I said, "I thought I could write." They asked why I didn't come as a singer. I replied, "I didn't think I could sing." They told me my songs had good lyrics, but that type was not what the public was looking for. They got me to sing several songs that other people had recorded and told me they would guarantee I would be in the top fifty with my first recording. They look for a certain type of voice, and I don't really know what, but by the time it goes through a half million dollars' worth of sound equipment, they can make a hound dog sound good! They gave me all the details, and I told them I would have to think about it.

I went home and talked it over with my wife and decided I didn't want that kind of life. First of all, they own you the first year or so until you get on a major label. And it's no wonder so many stars get hooked on prescription drugs. The public wants projection performance, not someone stepping out on the stage half asleep. By the time you travel across country, you are tired, so you might need an upper of some kind to get you out on that stage. And when you come off, you might need a downer to get you to sleep, so you can do the next show. If you make it big, you have no real social life. Someone is always watching you, and they usually have a camera.

I don't think I could handle a life like that. If I want to sit on the bench in the Walmart foyer and talk to people, I don't want people crowding around me for an autograph. I was satisfied with my life just the way it was. I had a beautiful family, good church family, and I had finally found the job that I enjoyed. And it was in my home state of Tennessee!

CHAPTER 29

When the Wind Blows, Raise Your Sail

I BECAME A heavy equipment operator. It was something that just came natural to me, and I was good at it. Thank You, Lord. I sure didn't need to be running all over the country, singing country music. I could stay home and write and sing gospel music and be much happier.

I had finally made a wise decision, but I'm still learning and still making poor decisions sometimes. Example: Lord, give me the music and words to a gospel song that will sell big time. I don't want a penny for it. I want to give all profits to the church. I really believe in prayer.

One night, sometime later, I woke up around two in the morning with the perfect song. I had never heard one so beautiful. Yes, Lord, You have answered my prayer once again. Thank You from the bottom of my heart. And just as soon as that clock goes off at five o'clock in the morning, I am going to jump right out of bed and write it down on paper.

Wrong. Such an idiot! Will I never learn I had waited on the Lord to give the perfect song, and He did, but I was too lazy to get out of bed and write it on paper. Not a word did I remember when the alarm clock went off—another lesson I learned the hard way.

Just the other night, in Bible study, the preacher said, "The Holy Spirit was like the wind, and we were like a ship on the sea. When that wind blows, only then does that ship move. The thing you have to remember to do is raise the sails." When the Holy Spirit moved, I was too lazy to get out of bed and raise the sails.

CHAPTER 30

Taking the Test

I HAVE BEEN tried and tested so many times. Sometimes, I pass the test. It seems most of the time, I fail. It grieves me to fail, but it teaches me to have stronger faith the next time I am faced with a trial.

There has been two times in my life in particular that made my faith stronger. I guess it is because I had nowhere else to turn. I am sorry to say that, but sometimes we don't have any alternative, and I thank God for making it so plain. When this happens, I can't find any way to rely on myself. I am probably not making much sense now, so I will just give you an example.

I had a pretty good job, and my wife was working also. We were doing fine, but we were spending it as fast as we earned it, just living from paycheck to paycheck. One day, I got hurt on the job, and I didn't report it. It got worse until I couldn't stand the pain. I finally went to the doctor. I had a ruptured disc in my lower back and had to be operated on. I was off work for three months without pay. My first day back to work was on a bulldozer for ten hours. I think that was a little too much for my first day back. I managed to work for several months, and one day, I fell on the job and hurt myself again.

This time, I reported it. They operated on me two more times and finally said I might never walk again. If I did walk, I would never be able to work again. I wouldn't be able to even pick up a pound of weight. Workman's comp cut me off and said I would have to file for disability. The doctor filed for me.

About the same time all of this was happening, my wife came home crying and said the company she worked for was moving to Mexico. We were in the middle of a recession, and there were no other jobs for her. We had a house payment and a car payment. Her unemployment wouldn't feed us, let alone make these payments. I was reading my Bible when she came home and told me these things. I just happened to be reading 2 Corinthians, chapter 12, verse 9: "But He said to me, My grace is sufficient for you, for my strength is made perfect in weakness." I showed her this. She read it, dried the tears from her eyes, and said, "You are right. The Lord will provide. It is out of our hands."

You see, we had no relatives who could help us financially. We had no money saved. We had no one whatsoever to turn to except the Lord. This is what I was getting at before. God let us get into a situation where we had no choice but to turn everything over to Him 100 percent.

We sometimes say that we have turned things over to God, but was it 100 percent? Or was it 50 percent? I can tell you from experience, you have to let God handle things 100 percent or not at all. Otherwise, you will just get in the way. My wife's unemployment ran out, and my disability had not started. We went for two years with no income whatsoever. To this day, I can't explain how we made it, earthly speaking that is. We asked the Lord to see us through, and He did.

A lot of times He will do it by putting before us a way to make money—not this time. We had no hand in it at all. He did it, and I cannot explain how. We never lost our house or even received a low mark on our credit score. We received no charity. I don't think we were even offered any. We never missed a meal or a payment. As far as our car payment was concerned, when we bought the car, it was in the contract that we had disability insurance included in the payments. We never told them to do that. And how it got in the contract, we did not know. We had made maybe six payments on it when I got hurt, and Ford Motor Company paid it off without any hassle at all. Lord, You really came through once again!

When all was done, we had an excellent credit rating. As far as my health was concerned, it was a hard battle, but I made it. I told the doctors and social security that if they thought I was going to lay on the couch, watch soap operas, and die, they better think again! I will do whatever is necessary to accomplish whatever I choose to do.

If I can't walk and do it, I will crawl. If I can't crawl, I'll get on my belly and slide like a snake. Some call me hardheaded—maybe so. I call it determined.

I am a firm believer that 75 percent of all pain is in your head, and I can prove that. If you are lying on your back, feeling like you are going to die, and suddenly your best friend from your younger days comes by, one you haven't seen in twenty years, and you start talking about the good times you had together—"Do you remember back when we used to do so and so?" "Oh yeah. Remember the time when…" (whatever comes to mind)—you get caught up in the good old days and you forget about the present, which holds your pain. After your friend leaves, your pain starts to creep back in. If you can keep your mind and fingers busy, you can stand about anything. I couldn't get out of my recliner, so what did I do? As I said before, through Jesus Christ, I can do anything. I took up embroidery. I've got pieces all over the country that I have given to people. It worked.

I don't get depressed. There are too many things to do, and a lot of them I haven't had a chance to do yet. As I progressed, I broadened my horizons. I made knives, shotgun stocks, furniture, and other wooden crafts.

Usually, when Christ heals, there is some kind of action that goes with it, which you must take. In the New Testament, after healing someone, Christ would say, "Go and…(whatever)."

God is so good, but He does not want you to be a freeloader. He expects you to put forth a little effort.

In my teachings in church, I always give this as an example of faith and effort. If you are hungry and have no food, don't lay down on the couch and say, "Lord, give me food" and then do nothing. You will most likely starve. On the other hand, if you say, "Lord, give me food," and then you get up and say, "Lord, I know You expect an action from me, so, Lord, I am going out that door. Please guide my steps toward the path I should take," and you then start walking down the road or street. And as you go by John Doe's house, he is sitting on the front porch, when suddenly he sees you, waves at you, and says, "Hey, come up and sit awhile." So you go up on the porch and sit awhile and talk with him. His wife opens the door and says, "John, your lunch is ready. Oh, hi, Jim, I didn't know you were here. Come on and have lunch with us. We have plenty and would enjoy having your company." Thank You, Lord! You have provided for me once again. The moral of the story is this: You can accomplish mighty things with a lot of faithful prayer and a little effort.

But the tests did not stop here.

CHAPTER 31

God of the Hills and the Valleys

WE SAW GOD move on our behalf and provide for us when no one else could, but we weren't on the mountaintop very long before something else happened.

My oldest daughter, which I talked about before and her miracle birth, became very sick. She was twenty-one. My wife took her to the doctor. The doctor took one look at her and said that she needed to get to Vanderbilt hospital as quick as possible. She had cancer.

It was caused from a drug called DES. I told you about the miraculous conception and birth. What we didn't realize was the doctor had decided to help God out. God didn't need his help. The doctor gave this new drug to my wife in case she might start to miscarry. Why can't we just trust God 100 percent? The doctor told us to pray. We prayed, and my wife conceived. Why did he give her that medicine, just in case? Folks, when you see God at work, get out of His way! You will only hinder things. If God wants you to do something, He will tell you too, and He will be specific. I insist on people talking to God and asking what He wants you to do, but you should always wait on His answer before you go into action.

The doctor at Vanderbilt told me, "I don't believe I can heal your daughter." My reply to him was, "You do what you think is right and leave the rest to the Lord. He can save her."

He said, "I am so glad to hear that, but if I said that myself, I could be sued."

Here again, I believe the doctor got in the way. He was a good man, but I believe he acted before he prayed. He ordered radiation. He said it was the maximum dose—thirty doses of it. It burned her so bad that it was pitiful. Words cannot describe it. It didn't change a thing either.

They had her in a broom closet with two inches of lead all around her after that. Her mom and I could go in that little room for five minutes out of a twenty-four-hour day and talk to her, but we couldn't see over the walls of lead. There were two sessions of that, which lasted one week each. That changed nothing. The doctor said there was only one thing left: surgery. She would probably die on the operating table. He let her come home, and he set the operation up for thirty days from that date.

I prayed and prayed, and finally the Lord spoke to me plainly, as if He were standing there beside me, which I knew now that He was. Sometimes we get so mealymouthed with our prayers. I don't even know if that is a word or not, but I think you will understand what I mean by it. The Bible says, we are to come boldly before the throne of God with our petitions. God said, "Speak up, son. Exactly what do you want?"

I said, "Okay, Lord. This is what I want. When my daughter goes back to the doctor in thirty days, let him look at her and say, 'Where did it go, Lord?' That way, no one can say man had anything to do with it, only God!"

He said, "All you had to do was ask."

I have never had such a feeling of relief.

I was in a gospel group at that time. We went all over, playing and singing, and everywhere I went, I told my story. The word spread, and so did prayers over several different states. I told them all how my daughter would be healed on a certain date. I had some to tell me they appreciated my faith, but what if God decided to change His mind? I told them, "God does not change His mind. But if it were possible, then He would come to me and say, 'Jim, I have decided to take your daughter's life.' In a case like that, I would say, 'Take her, Lord. She's Yours.'" Abraham, in the Bible, had to make the same choice. If I would have said no because I can't live without her, He would have said, "Don't tell me. I am still in control."

When the thirty days were up, we got up that morning, and my wife said, "I dread today."

I said, "Why?"

She said, "You really believe the cancer is gone, don't you?"

I replied, "I don't just believe. I know."

My wife and my sister took her up there that day. I went ahead with my daily routine. That late afternoon, they pulled up in the front of the house and got out with smiles from ear to ear! My wife said, "Guess what?"

I confidently replied, "I know what!"

She said the doctors said, if it were not for the burns on her from radiation, he would say that she never had cancer!

She has had a lot of trouble over the years because of the radiation, but over thirty years later, she is still cancer-free. I hate to say I learned a lot at her expense, but I did. I learned what faith is. I learned that faith really could move mountains, and the tests and trials helped us to endure the valleys.

In my younger days, I searched for a job that I enjoyed. It's understandable now why the Lord wanted me to be a heavy equipment operator.

Using the machines, *I* could move a lot of dirt, mountains of dirt, rock, rubble. *I* could change the landscape, create roads where roads were not. The Lord used this to teach me that I had no control over this mountain. I needed to just get out of the way and leave my bulldozer at home because I wouldn't need it! God has moved the mountains and obstacles for me all of my life! I know He will continue to do so. I am never surprised, yet I am amazed.

Why can't we just take our burdens to the feet of Jesus and leave them there? He knows what to do with them. We complain about life. But without being tested by the world, we could never have the relationship with our Savior like He intended it to be. We won't be able to appreciate the mountaintops without the valleys.

I always tell people, "You don't know what faith is until you have been through a little fire. I can tell you these things because I've been there. I know what faith is."

CHAPTER 32

Turn That Frown Upside Down

HAD I NOT been brought up hard and fast, I don't think I could have withstood some of the things I have had to endure. I am glad I wasn't brought up with a silver spoon in my mouth. Oh, it was rough, but it made me a survivor and a better Christian.

I don't have much pity on people who have a few disappointments in life and just lay down and start whining and gives up. Take these bad times and turn them around and learn from them and grow stronger. It's the same thing as a smile. A smile is a frown that you have turned upside down. You are a much more beautiful person if you go through life with a smile, rather than a frown.

My life has been full of ups and downs from the day I was born. I look back and see where God has always been in charge. I didn't always realize this at the time though. The reason I am writing this today is in hopes that someone will read my message and turn their lives around without having to go through what I have. I have endured a lot of pain and suffering so I can tell others about it and show them how to make their lives better.

Jesus Christ gave His life so ours could be made whole. I beg the people who read this book to please take heed. God has sent me to be a witness. If you will ask the Holy Spirit to give you clarity and then study your Bible, you will understand what I am trying to tell you.

I have been able to do some of my most powerful witnessing while in the hospital. Once when my appendix ruptured, I was sent to Vanderbilt hospital in Nashville. It happened on a Wednesday night, and I thought it was a kidney stone and refused to go to the hospital, even though the pain was excruciating. I told my wife I would go on Monday if I didn't pass a stone by then. My youngest daughter came over Saturday night, took one look at me, and told her mother that Daddy would not be here Monday if he didn't get help now, so they took me to the hospital against my will.

Sunday morning, at six, I was in surgery. It had been like eighty hours since my appendix had ruptured. The doctors said, after twenty-four hours, I was supposed to be dead. The Lord was not through with me yet. I think every doctor in the hospital must have come to look at me. They said there were two things that couldn't be explained: First of all, appendicitis, after forty years of age, was almost unheard of. I was over sixty. Number two was, I couldn't live that long with a ruptured appendix. They said that it had to be because a higher power was watching over me.

The door for witnessing was wide open. People were coming to my room, asking for prayer—from doctors to floor sweepers. I couldn't possibly concentrate on my situation of agonizing pain. The Lord kept me busy with my work for Him. Through all my pain, it was still a glorious time just to know the Lord could use me as a tool, even on my supposed deathbed. Don't ever give up. There is always work to be done for the Lord. And while you are doing it, you keep your mind off your situations—mind over matter. These people's spiritual life had to take priority over my physical life.

At age sixty-five, I had a heart attack. They said it was major. I said it was minor. They put five stints in my heart. I always try to have a positive attitude toward things. Even though I was in a lot of pain, I tried to smile. I asked the helicopter pilot if I could make the take off when they took me to Nashville. He laughed and said, "Maybe on the way back." I watched my family standing by the pad, crying as the helicopter took off. I wondered if I would ever see them again on this side of heaven. It didn't matter really. I knew that I would see them in heaven someday. Everything went like clockwork. I only stayed in the hospital a couple of days. Here again, the doctors said it was a miraculous recovery. I think, by the hand of God, I left a positive mark on everyone from the ER to the helicopter crew to the hospital. If not, I would have two more chances before the week was up.

A couple of days after I got home, I had to go back to the ER. They said my gall bladder was about to rupture. Back to Nashville

I went, this time in an ambulance. They had a surgeon waiting on me when I got there. He came in, looked at my records, and said, "I wouldn't touch this man with a ten-foot pole. You didn't tell me he just had a heart attack. If I punch a hole in his stomach, he will bleed to death from the inside because of all the blood thinner in him." They called in another doctor who said, "I'll do it, but I will have to do it the old-fashioned way. If I cut you open, I can control the bleeding."

I said, "Doc, I won't tell you how to do your job if you promise not to tell me how to run a bulldozer."

Everything, once again, went textbook smooth. I went home again, only to go back to the ER a day or so later with a kidney stone. By the way, in case you have never had one, it is one of the most painful things there is. All these things happened in a seven-day period. They all got to know me by my first name in two different hospitals, an ambulance, and a helicopter. I don't know about some of the people, but I know some of the doctors, and they still talk about that week, and they also tell other people, who have all agreed, that it was miracle after miracle.

A few years later, I had some blood work done, and they told me my bilirubin levels were elevated. Who ever heard of bilirubin? They said I had a gall stone.

"Impossible!" I exclaimed. "I haven't had a gall bladder in ten years!"

It turned out that a gall stone lodged in the lower part of my liver. Don't ask me how it got there. They couldn't explain it unless there was a grain of sand left in me from my gall bladder surgery. No sweat, they are going to pull it out with a probe, just day surgery and go home. Wrong! They tore a hole in the wall of my pancreas. Why do these off-the-wall things keep happening to me? I spent eleven days in the hospital and then came home with a pick line in me for two more weeks. Here again, the hospital staff were amazed. I lived and was able to keep a good attitude. I met a lot of people and got to be a witness to them. You don't have to be a pastor of a great church or even a good speaker to be a witness. You just have to be willing to let the Lord use you, then people can see Him through you.

They say actions speak louder than words. In a lot of cases, I think that is true. There are many kinds of pain. Physical and mental are two of them, and I hate pain. But if I can be a positive witness for the Lord by enduring pain, so be it. This life is so short compared to eternity with the Lord. I am now seventy-eight, and I went to the doctor a couple of months ago for a yearly checkup. He said he didn't like what he was seeing. Three days later, he wanted to run a heart cath on me. I might have to have another stint in my heart. When he checked me, he said I was a walking dead man—pretty plainly spoken!

My widow-maker artery was 99 percent blocked, and another artery was 98 percent blocked. That's odd for someone who does not have high cholesterol. I actually felt relieved. I'm about to go home, where there is no pain and suffering. Several years ago, I told the Lord I would do whatever He wanted me to do, but I had one request, if it is in His will. (You don't make deals with God and that certainly wasn't what I was trying to do.) I have seen people have such a long-drawn-out death, and the family went through agony sitting by the bedside, watching daily as one slipped just a tiny bit further away day by day, possibly month by month. There is probably nothing worse that a family can endure. I told the Lord, "I am used to pain, but please don't put my family through that because of me. If it be in your will, Lord. Just let me fall over dead or go to sleep and not wake up." When they told me my heart was in such bad shape, I thought, *Yes, Lord. You are about to give me my request.* I told the doctor I didn't want the operation.

I thought my wife was going to finish the job…right then and there! I knew I probably sounded selfish, but it was her and the rest of my family that I was thinking about. My cardiologist sat down by my bed and talked to me in a very Christian way. He said, "Jim, the Lord didn't send you to Nashville to die. He sent you here to get well. You have another ten or twelve years ahead of you that can be productive."

That made sense, so I told him to set it up. In my mind, I was thinking that I would pray about it. And if the Lord didn't want me to have the operation, I would cancel it. In the meantime, two real good preacher friends of mine talked to me over the phone and confirmed the doctor was right, so I agreed. Everything went like clockwork. The surgeon said I would stay for a couple of days in ICU. I stayed a half of a day. He said one to two weeks in the hospital. Three and a half days later, I went home. Lord, You still got something for me to do. I don't know what just yet, but I am listening, Lord. I know You will reveal it to me when the time is right. I just have to remember not to get anxious and get ahead of You. I am on Your timetable and not mine. I do enjoy working for You though, and I am always amazed at how and why You have used me. We are all uniquely made and special in the eyes of God, so please don't ever think God can't use you. He doesn't ask for the equipped, He asks for someone who is willing to let Him do the equipping.

CHAPTER 33

Crooked Justice

THE NEWS JUST told a terrible story about some rogue cops in Memphis who beat a young man until he died three days later. It brings back a lot of memories that I have tried so hard to forget. I wasn't going to write about that, but now I feel I should.

I believe it was 1975. I had worked all day and was walking down the street in Chattanooga when someone whistled. I turned around to see who it was. There were two cops coming toward me and yelled really smart, like, "Hold it right there!" I thought, *Who are they talking to?* I looked around, and there was no one else around but me. I turned back and said, "Who, me?"

"Yes you!" they exclaimed. They walked up to me, and one of them reached into his pocket and pulled out a coin and flipped it to the sidewalk and said in a very demanding voice, "Pick it up!"

I said, "Mister, I have a job and work hard for my money, and I don't go around picking up money off the street. It's your coin, and you threw it down there. So if you want it, you pick it up." In an instance, I was hit with a blackjack just above my left ear. I was young and quite fast in those days. And by the time the blackjack hit me, I had a hold on his right arm, so I took him down with me as I fell. I weighed about 140 pounds. Now I had someone who looked like a linebacker for Green Bay on top of me, trying to hit me with that blackjack again. I somehow got my right arm around his neck and pulled his head down to my chest with everything I had. That way, he could not get a good lick in on me.

The next thing I knew, there were cops coming from everywhere! Five of them got me up and took my boots off me and threw me in the back of a squad car so hard that I thought my head was going to go through the opposite door. Two of the cops got in the front seat, and away we went. I couldn't understand what was happening! They were taking me to jail, and I hadn't done anything wrong! They stopped the squad car, but we weren't at the jail. They stopped in a back alley. Another squad car pulled in and stopped next to us. There were three officers in that car. They all got out and drug me out into the alley and started beating me with their fists and billy clubs while I was lying back across the hood of one of the cars. Finally, I was able to get off the hood, only to land on my back on the street. That's when they started stomping me and kicking me. I thought I was going to die at any moment. Finally, they stopped and put me back in the squad car.

This time, they took me to jail. I couldn't walk, so the jailer set the phone down in the floor and let me have my one phone call. I called my wife, and she got my best friend, and he put his property up for bail money to get me released.

I got a lawyer, who turned out to be the ex-DA. Boy, can I pick them. We went to court, and the only thing he said was, "My client pleads not guilty." They wouldn't even let me tell my side of the story. The prosecuting attorney said, "Judge, this man is accused of choking a police officer and kicking him between the legs." Nothing was said about the three other cops and how five of them beat me. The DA said, "Judge, I suggest thirty days for disorderly conduct and eleven months and twenty-nine days for assault and battery of a police officer."

The judge said, "So be it. I am tired of this kind of thing going on."

They took me out of the courtroom to the hall, and the DA said, "Marlow, I understand you have a job and a wife and two small children at home."

I replied, "That's right."

He said, "Tell me, Marlow, what is your wife and kids going to do while you are in jail for twelve months and twenty-nine days?"

That was a blow below the belt. I said, "I don't know."

He told me that if I would go back in the courtroom and tell the judge that I admit my guilt so I couldn't go to the chief and squeal about them beating me up that he would see that I never spent a day in jail.

My lawyer told him that he needed a private moment with his client. He took me over in a corner and talked. He said, "Jim, I know it hurts bad, but you have no other choice. If you don't do as they say, you will go to the city jail for five days before you are transported to the county jail. You will never leave the city jail alive. They will stage a tempted jailbreak and kill you. They are not going to let you go to the chief."

I told him, "Okay."

We went back to the courtroom, and the DA said, "Judge, this man has something to say."

I told him I was guilty as charged.

The DA said, "Since he admits his quilt, I suggest we let him off, judge."

The judge agreed and wrote, "Out on good behavior," on a release form. It's pretty obvious it was a corrupt police department and a kangaroo court system. The difference between me and Tyre Nichols is, I lived, and he didn't. The circumstances were pretty much the same. I tell this story to say, race has nothing to do with it. If a cop is bad, he is just looking for another head to bash. I am White, and those five cops were white. Those five who beat Tyre were all Black, and he was Black. My sympathy goes out to his family. May God give them peace that only He can give, along with the strength they have to find. We are all brothers and sisters, though the skin of our body may be a different color. But there are some who make a career out of trying to convince others we are different, including a lot of news people. Bad news sells better, just like gossip is more interesting than the truth. It took me a long time to get over that ordeal, not only physically but more mentally. Every time I saw a blue uniform, I thought of what happened, and I could feel the hate start to build in me for a long time. A period of time passed, and I dedicated my life to God. By His help, I was able to let it go. I don't even remember their names anymore.

I have found that very few cops are bad. It only takes a few to damage the image of all though. Some of my best friends today are police officers. There is an old saying that it only takes one rotten apple to stink up the whole bushel.

EPILOGUE

Conclusion

LIFE IS SO full of ups and downs, joy and sadness, pain and sufferings. I have had my share though. I have only mentioned a few. The things I have mentioned are certainly just a small part of my life, and I am not asking for sympathy. I have had a lot of happy times also. The point I am trying to make is be happy, no matter what situation you find yourself in. Be grateful for the things you have. No matter what you think, you don't have, or how much pain there is in your life, just remember to look around, and you will see others who have less possessions or more pain.

If your knee hurts, look around. You will find someone who doesn't have a leg. With my bank account, you probably couldn't get out of the state of Tennessee, yet I am rich. I have so much more than I need and am so thankful for it. All I have to do is think back to where I came from, and I realize how rich I am today. Someone gave me the best complement some time back, but it was actually meant as a slur. They said, "Jim, if you had anything, you would just give it away." I said, "Who needs money when they have everything?"

I am very content with what I have. It all belongs to God, and He lets me use whatever I need. My heavenly Father has always been there for me, and He has taught me to be positive in a negative situation.

You, men out there, be real men. Be the spiritual leader of your home as God made you to be. Take care of family with your life and, by all means, get your leadership abilities from God. Ladies, help your husbands to be all they can be, a real God-fearing man. Stand by him. Men, treat your wife with the highest respect. She is the most precious jewel you will ever have. Both of you must work hard at everything you do in your relationship with each other, your children, your home, and especially your walk with the Lord. If both will always be willing to give 100 percent of yourself and expect nothing in return from the other, your marriage will be a marriage made in heaven. What a role for your children who are always watching. You might even find yourself celebrating a golden wedding anniversary as I have, plus five and looking for many more, not to mention three wonderful children and a bunch of grandchildren and a few great grandchildren…well, only one great-grandchild, but I am thinking positively!

Back to the title of this book. Was I poor white trash or just someone without a firm foundation? At any rate, I found that firm foundation and built on it. I was a pauper, and now I am a child of the King. Thank You, my dear heavenly Father!

To conclude, I haven't tried to put this book in chronological order, so if some of the dates and times don't come out exactly as they should, forgive me. I am old, and time means very little to me anymore. The events have happened as I have told them.

May God bless each person who reads these words, and may these words help direct someone to a better life.

ACKNOWLEDGMENTS

THANK YOU TO Barry Rhoads, my friend and former pastor who first told me I should write a book; two of my granddaughters, Josie Payne and Katie Payne, who would come to my house and say, "Papa, tell us some more stories of how you grew up"; and last but certainly not the least is my niece, Teresa Pedigo, who typed and edited this book, as well as encouraged me constantly. I could not have done it without her. I will also tell you this: she said she was looking for something she could do for the Lord, and when she read my rough copy, she knew this was it. Thank You, Lord, and thank you, Teresa.

ABOUT THE AUTHOR

JIMMY MARLOW IS not an author of books but has written numerous songs.

He is self-taught on guitar and leads singing at his church.

He doesn't have degrees behind his name, but he has experienced so much in life and has been led by God to share his story at this time, in his almost eighty years of life, in the hopes that he can help someone else who is going through the struggles of life to draw their strength from the Lord and find their hope in the Lord.

He still operates heavy equipment.

He has been married to the love of his life for fifty-six and a half years and is a father of three, grandfather of nine, and great-grandfather of one (at this time).

He wholeheartedly enjoys his time with his family and friends and is always entertaining. He is very active in church and rarely meets a stranger. He is truly rich.

Printed in the USA
CPSIA information can be obtained
at www.ICGtesting.com
CBHW031611131124
17315CB00023B/442